BEST
HOMEMADE
PIZZA
GOURMET'S
COOKBOOK

Enjoy 25 creative and Fast To Make
Gourmet's Pizzas Any Time Of The Day.

Table of contents

Chicken Garlic Pizza

Chicken, Bacon & Strawberry Pizza

Meatball Pizza

Pizza Cubano

Pepperoni & Cheese Tortilla Pizza

Avocado & Salmon Tortilla Pizza

Shrimp & Basil Pesto Pizza

Chicken & Bacon-Basil Pesto Pizza

Chicken-Broccoli Garlic Bread Pizza

Introduction

Who doesn't love pizza? Pizza is the ultimate food. It is quick to make an easy clean-up meal, and always a hit for any occasion be it family, social feasts, parties, and night out with a friend. Pizza is so yummy that it is the favorite in every group, be it kids or adults. Its versatility makes this tasty comfort food perfect to serve as a full meal, snack or dessert.

This cookbook catalogs two comprehensive collections of delicious gourmet vegetarian and meaty pizza recipes respectively that can be prepared at home with common pantry ingredients. These pizzas are incredibly delicious that you will stop buying ready make pizzas from the market and will lose your desire to order a takeout. From vegan to gluten-free pizza, vegetarian to meaty pizza, bake to grilled pizza, tortilla to whole-wheat base, in addition to delicious options, you will find something for yourself.

Of course, the key to a delicious pizza is pizza dough. For your convenience, 16-ounce pizza dough is directly added to each recipe. Follow the direction of the recipe below to whip your batch of pizza dough.

INGREDIENTS

5.8 ounces / 165g whole-wheat flour / all-purpose flour / bread flour
½ teaspoon salt
1/8 teaspoon sugar
1 teaspoon dry active yeast
4 fluid ounces / 120ml warm water
1 ½ teaspoons olive oil

DIRECTIONS

- Pour warm water in a small bowl, add yeast and sugar, stir until combine and let it rest for 10 minutes or until the mixture is foamy.
- In the meantime place the flour and salt in a food processor and pulse for 4-5 times until mix well.
- Add foamy yeast mixture and 1 ½ tablespoon oil and process again until the dough comes together. If the dough is too dry, mix 1-2 tablespoons of water and if the dough is too wet mix 1-2 tablespoons of flour.
- An alternate way to prepare dough is to make it in a bread machine by adding all the ingredients into the machine's basket. An

electric stand mixer can also be used. The end product will be a sticky dough.

- Transfer the dough onto a clean working space, dusted with flour. Knead dough for 5-6 times or until it's firm and elastic, and shape it into a ball. Then transfer the dough to a greased bowl with oil, cover it with a clean towel or plastic wrap and let it rest in a warm environment for 45-60 minutes or until it doubles in size.
- When the dough has expanded, return to the working space, punch it down and knead again for 4-5 times. Return dough to its bowl, cover and let it rest in a warm place for another 30-45 minute or until it double in size.
- Now at this stage, the dough can be kept in the freezer. Place the dough ball in a resealable plastic bag and freeze dough in the freezer for up to 3 months.
- For using the dough, thaw overnight completely and stretch into desired pizza crust sized.

Feel free to play around with the basic recipe of pizza crust and make your own pizza with delicious toppings.

Indeed no food in a world is cheap to prepare than a pizza.

Healthy Vegetarian Pizzas

Stuffed Waffle Pizza

Simple to make, gluten free pepperoni waffle pizza is amazingly delicious and is a perfect a quick fix breakfast and snack.

Yield: About 1 waffle
Total Time: 25 minutes

INGREDIENTS
1 gluten free waffle, frozen
3 tablespoons pizza sauce
6 slices of pepperoni
2 tablespoons fat-free shredded mozzarella cheese

DIRECTIONS

- Switch on broiler and preheat.
- Switch on the toaster, set to medium heat setting, place a waffle and heat for 2 minutes or until thoroughly warm and crisp.
- Spread pizza sauce onto warm waffle, then top with pepperoni slices and spread evenly with cheese.
- Place waffle in a baking tray and place in broiler for 2-3 minutes or until cheese melts and the top is a nice golden brown.

NUTRITIONAL INFORMATION PER SERVING:

250 Cal, 4g total fat (2 g sat. fat), 0 mg chol., 415 mg sodium, 15g carb., 3 g fiber, 6 g protein.

Two-Tomato Pizza

This flavor-packed pizza is a vibrant combination of fresh plum tomatoes. It is low fat and turns out delicious with just five ingredients.

Yield: About 1 pizza
Total Time: 40 minutes

INGREDIENTS

1 medium fresh yellow tomato
2 medium fresh red tomatoes
2 tablespoons olive oil
½ teaspoon salt
12 ounces / 340g frozen pizza dough, thawed

DIRECTIONS

- Switch on the baking oven, set the temperature at 475 degrees F and let it preheat.

- In the meantime, grease a baking tray with oil generously and set aside until when needed.
- Fill a medium saucepan half full with water, place it over medium-high flame and bring to boil.
- Blanch tomato. For this, make a shallow mark like X on the bottom of the tomato and submerge into boiling water. Cook for 30 seconds and then using slotted spoon, transfer to an ice water bath and leave for 30 seconds. Then using a sharp knife, peel away the skin from the tomato.
- Blanch red tomatoes in the same manner and then peel away the skin.
- Remove seeds from tomatoes and puree in a blender separately.
- Place dough on a baking tray and shape it into a 9 by 13-inch crust. Even spread yellow tomatoes mixture over 1/3 length of pizza crust and then spread red tomato mixture over the remaining crust.
- Drizzle with oil, sprinkle with salt and then place pan into the oven.
- Bake pizza for 20-25 minutes or until crust is nicely golden brown and top is brown.
- Remove baked pizza from oven, let it cool for 5 minutes and then slice to serve.

NUTRITIONAL INFORMATION PER SERVING:

156 Cal, 6.6 g total fat, 0 mg chol., 120 mg sodium, 16 g carb., 1 g fiber, 8 g protein.

Basil Pesto & Tomato Pizza

Spend weekend night by making this classic Italian tomato pizza that pairs well with bold flavor of basil pesto.

Yield: About 1 pizza
Total Time: 30 minutes

INGREDIENTS

16 ounces / 450g frozen pizza dough, thawed
3 medium tomatoes
6 ounces / 170g fat-free shredded mozzarella cheese
3 tablespoons basil pesto
¾ teaspoon salt
½ teaspoon ground black pepper

DIRECTIONS

- Switch on the baking oven, set the temperature at 500 degrees F and let it preheat.
- In the meantime, grease a 14-inch pizza pan with oil generously and set aside until require.
- Cut each tomato into 1/8-inch slices.
- Transfer dough onto a clean working space, dusted with flour lightly. Pat dough and using rolling pin shape dough into 12 inch diameter round crust. Roll crust, then unroll over prepared pizza pan and gently press it to the edges.
- Spread pesto evenly over crust and leave 1 inch edge. Sprinkle with cheese and then evenly arrange tomato slices.
- Season with salt and black pepper and then place pan into the oven.
- Bake pizza for 10-12 minutes or until crust is nicely golden brown and top is brown.
- Remove baked pizza from oven, let cool for 5 minutes and then slice to serve.

NUTRITIONAL INFORMATION PER SERVING:

228 Cal, 10.5 g total fat, 12 mg chol., 207 mg sodium, 22 g carb., 2 g fiber, 12 g protein.

Eggplant & Parmesan Cheese

This healthy pizza is packed with the flavors of crunchy eggplant slices and parmesan cheese. Serve this pizza with a green salad and have it even for breakfast.

Yield: About 1 pizza
Total Time: 50 minutes

INGREDIENTS

16 ounces / 450g frozen pizza dough, thawed
16 ounces / 450g eggplants
1 egg white
8 fluid ounces / 236ml pasta sauce
8 ounces / 180g fat-free shredded mozzarella cheese
2 ounces / 45g cup grated parmesan cheese
2 ounces / 60g breadcrumbs, seasoned

DIRECTIONS

- Switch on the baking oven, set the temperature at 375 degrees F and let it preheat.
- In the meantime, grease a 14" inch pizza pan and set aside until necessary.
- Peel eggplants and cut into even slices. Dip each slice into egg white, cover with crumbs and then place onto the prepared baking tray.
- Place the baking tray into an oven and bake for 10 minutes until both sides nicely turn brown.
- Remove eggplant slices from oven, switch temperature of the oven to 400 degrees F and let heat.
- Transfer dough onto a clean working space, dusted with flour. Pat dough and using rolling pin shape dough into12 inch diameter round crust. Roll crust, then unroll the prepared pizza pan over and gently press it to the edges.
- Spread pizza sauce over crust, leave about 1-inch edge. Arrange baked eggplant slices, cover with cheeses and place the pan into the oven.
- Bake pizza for 12-15 minutes or until crust and top is nicely golden brown.
- Remove baked pizza from oven, let it cool for 5 minutes and then slice to serve.

NUTRITIONAL INFORMATION PER SERVING:

285 Cal, 11 g total fat (4.4 g sat. fat), 74.5 mg chol., 745 mg sodium, 35.7 g carb., 7.5 g fiber, 19.9 g protein.

Vegan Green Pizza

This pizza is clean, meatless, dairy-free and low calorie. Creamy kale pesto, olives, broccoli, chickpeas, artichoke hearts, onion, and nuts make this vegan pizza a tasty and healthy meal.

Yield: About 1 pizza
Total Time: 30 minutes

INGREDIENTS

16 ounces / 470g fresh kale, divided
½ teaspoon salt, divided
½ teaspoon ground black pepper, divided
1 tablespoons olive oil
4 ounces sunflower seeds
2 teaspoons minced garlic
1 tablespoon lemon juice
16 ounces / 450g frozen whole-wheat pizza dough, thawed
4 ounces / 115g chickpeas, cooked
4 ounces / 115g broccoli florets

1 small white onion
10 kalamata olives
5 artichokes hearts
2 ounces / 60g pine nuts
2 ounces / 60g basil leaves
2 ounces / 60g mint leaves

DIRECTIONS

- Switch on the baking oven, set the temperature at 428 degrees F and preheat.
- In the meantime, grease a 14-inch pizza pan with oil and set aside until necessary.
- Chop kale leaves and place half of the kale in a blender, reserve remaining kale for topping.
- Into a blender, add garlic, lemon juice, sunflower seeds, ¼ teaspoon ground black pepper, remaining oil and salt, and pulse until smooth. Tip pesto into a bowl and set aside until necessary.
- Transfer the dough to a clean working space, dusted with flour. Pat dough using rolling pin which will shape dough into a 12-inch diameter round crust. Roll crust, then unroll it over prepared pizza pan and gently press it to the edges.
- Place pan into the oven for 3 minutes or until crust is nicely golden brown.
- While the crust bakes, peel an onion and cut into thin rings. Pit olives and cut each into half. Cut each artichoke heart in half.
- Remove pizza pan from oven, flip crust upside-down and then evenly spread with prepared kale pesto, leave 1-inch edge.

- Spread reserve kale leaves over crust, then arrange broccoli florets, scatter with chickpeas, top with artichoke hearts, olives, onion rings and nuts.
- Drizzle oil over crust, season with remaining black pepper and return pan to oven.
- Bake pizza for 7-10 minutes or until crust is nicely golden brown.
- Remove baked pizza from oven, let cool for 5 minutes, garnish with basil and mint leaves and then slice to serve.

NUTRITIONAL INFORMATION PER SERVING:

283 Cal, 14 g total fat (4 g sat. fat), 19 mg chol., 512 mg sodium, 33 g carb., 3g fiber, 15 g protein.

Chinese Pizza with Tofu

This pizza is a vegetarian version of Chinese chicken pizza. This Chinese pizza has tamari-ginger & garlic flavored tofu and hoisin sauce. Red pepper boast flavored, and green onions and cilantro add freshness.

Yield: About 1 pizza
Total Time: 65 minutes

INGREDIENTS
14 ounces fat-free tofu, firmed
1 tablespoon sesame oil, and more as needed
1 tablespoon gluten-free tamari
1 teaspoon minced garlic
2 teaspoons minced ginger
1 small red pepper
2 tablespoons chopped green onion
1 tablespoon chopped cilantro
1 tablespoon hoisin sauce

8 ounces / 225g frozen gluten-free pizza dough, thawed

DIRECTIONS

- In a medium sized bowl stir together sesame oil, tamari, garlic and ginger until it combines well.
- Press tofu in a tofu pressure for 15 minutes or until water is out and then cut into even slices.
- Add tofu into sesame oil mixture and toss until it becomes coated. Let's marinate for 45 minutes.
- In the meantime, chop red pepper.
- Switch on the baking oven, set the temperature at 350 degrees F and let it preheat. Grease a 9-inch pizza pan and set it aside until necessary
- Transfer dough onto a clean working space, dusted with flour. Pat dough and use a rolling pin to shape dough into a 7-inch diameter round crust. Roll crust, then unroll it over prepared pizza pan and gently press it to the edges.
- Place a non-stick wok over medium flame, add two tablespoons sesame oil and heat until hot. Add marinated tofu in a single layer and sauté for 5-7 minutes per side or until it turns golden brown on all sides. Cook remaining tofu slices in the same manner and then crumble.
- Spread hoisin sauce onto pizza crust, leave 1-inch edge, spread with tofu and sprinkle with red pepper.
- Place pizza pan into oven, switch temperature to 450 degrees F and bake for 10-12 minutes

or until the crust is nicely golden brown and pepper is tender.

- Remove baked pizza from oven, let it cool for 5 minutes, garnish with cilantro and green onion and then slice to serve.

NUTRITIONAL INFORMATION PER SERVING:

264 Cal, 8 g total fat (1.2 g sat. fat), 45 mg chol., 405 mg sodium, 37.8 g carb., 3.6 g fiber, 10.4 g protein.

Barbecue Tofu Pizza

Barbecue tofu pizza is a delicious pizza that is free from meat and cheese. Moreover, it tastes exactly like the real barbecue chicken pizza.

Yield: About 1 pizza
Total Time: 35 minutes

INGREDIENTS

- 14 ounces fat-free tofu, firmed
- ½ teaspoon salt
- ¼ teaspoon ground black pepper
- 2 ounces / 38g cornstarch
- 2 fluid ounces / 60ml olive oil
- 16 ounces / 450g frozen pizza dough, thawed
- 8 fluid ounces / 235ml barbecue sauce
- 1 small red onion
- 13 ounces fat-free shredded mozzarella cheese
- 2 ounces chopped cilantro

DIRECTIONS

- Press tofu in a tofu pressure for 15 minutes or until water is out and then cut into even slices.
- In a bowl combine cornstarch, salt and black pepper and then evenly cover tofu slices.
- Place a non-stick wok over medium-high flame, add oil and heat until hot. Add covered tofu slices in a single layer to wok and cook for 10 minutes per side or until it turns golden brown on all sides.
- Cook the remaining tofu slices in the same manner and place it in a bowl. Add half of the barbecue sauce and toss until it becomes coated.
- Switch on the baking oven, set temperature at 375 degrees F and let preheat.
- In the meantime, grease a 16-inch pizza pan with oil.
- Peel onion and cut into thin rings.
- Transfer dough onto a clean working space, dusted with flour. Pat dough using a rolling pin and shape the dough into a 14 inch diameter round crust. Roll crust, then unroll over prepared pizza pan and gently press it to the edges.
- Spread remaining barbecue sauce over crust, leave 1-inch edge, top evenly with tofu mixture and arrange onion slices.
- Sprinkle cheese over crust and place pan into the oven to bake for 10-12 minutes or until crust and top is nicely golden brown.
- Remove baked pizza from oven, let cool for 5 minutes, sprinkle with ¼ teaspoon salt, garnish with cilantro and slice to serve.

NUTRITIONAL INFORMATION PER SERVING:

213.5 Cal, 5 g total fat(1.2 g sat. fat), 45 mg chol., 552.5 mg sodium, 32 g carb., 3.75 g fiber, 8.5 g protein.

Tempeh Caesar Salad Pizza

Tempeh is a great alternative for meat if you don't like tofu. This pizza is a vegan version of a traditional light chicken Caesar salad pizza. It's loaded with incredible flavors of vegetarian ranch dressing, tempeh and healthy lettuce and avocado.

Yield: About 1 pizza
Total Time: 45 minutes

INGREDIENTS

- 1 medium avocado
- 16 ounces / 450g frozen pizza dough, thawed
- 24 ounces chopped lettuce
- 3 teaspoons minced garlic
- 8 ounces / 220g soy mayonnaise
- 1 tablespoon soy butter
- 3 tablespoons nutritional yeast
- ½ teaspoon onion powder
- ½ teaspoon ground black pepper
- ¼ teaspoon ground oregano

½ teaspoon soy sauce
6 fluid ounces / 180ml soy milk
4 smoked tempeh bacon slices

DIRECTIONS

- Switch on the baking oven, set the temperature at 400 degrees F and let it preheat.
- Grease a 14-inch pizza pan with oil and set aside until needed.
- While the oven heats, prepare the ranch dressing. Place a medium saucepan, add one tablespoon oil and heat until hot. Add garlic and sauté for 1-2 minutes until it turns to golden brown and fragrant.
- Add mayonnaise, butter, yeast, onion powder, black pepper, oregano, soy sauce. Then using a whisker, stir all the sauce ingredients and then slowly whisk in milk until sauce reaches to desire thickness.
- Tip sauce in a large bowl and place in refrigerator until chill and the little bit firm.
- Now, transfer the dough to a clean working space, dusted with flour. Pat the dough by using the rolling pin, shape dough into 12-inch diameter round crust. Roll crust, then unroll over prepared pizza pan and gently press it to the edges.
- Poke crust using a fork, place pan into the oven and bake for 15-20 minutes until crust is nicely golden brown and crispy.
- While crust bakes, chop tempeh. Place a medium sized frying pan, heat one tablespoon of olive oil and cook tempeh slices in batches

for 5-8 minutes or until evenly golden brown on all sides.
- Then transfer cooked tempeh slices onto a cutting board, then cut into strips and chop.
- Peel avocado, core and dice.
- Removed baked crust from oven and assemble the pizza. Spread prepared ranch dressing until crust is covered, leave 1-inch edge. Top with chopped lettuce, cooked tempeh bacon, avocado and drizzle with more ranch dressing.
- Remove baked pizza from oven, let cool for 5 minutes and then sprinkle lightly with crushed red pepper and slice to serve.

NUTRITIONAL INFORMATION PER SERVING:

300 Cal, 6 g total fat (1g sat. fat), 43 mg chol., 952 mg sodium, 28 g carb., 3 g fiber, 25 g protein.

Roasted Vegetables & Tempeh Pizza

This vegan pizza is healthy, nutritious and has low calories. It is meat-free, dairy free and super delicious. It is made from simple whole-wheat dough, loaded with roasted vegetables and tempeh. You won't even miss cheese and meat in this pizza.

Yield: About 1 pizza
Total Time: 90 minutes

INGREDIENTS

16 ounces / 450g frozen whole-wheat pizza dough, thawed
2 tablespoons olive oil, and more as needed
6 fluid ounces / 170g tomato puree
¼ teaspoon Sriracha sauce
¼ teaspoon garlic powder
¼ teaspoon liquid smoke
½ cup eggplant slices

½ cup zucchini slices
5 tempeh slices
8.3 ounces / 500g cremini mushrooms
¼ teaspoon paprika powder

DIRECTIONS

- Switch on the baking oven, set the temperature at 375 degrees F and let it preheat.
- Grease a 14-inch pizza pan with oil and set aside until needed.
- In a medium sized mixing bowl, place tomato puree, add Sriracha sauce, garlic powder and liquid smoke and using a whisker stir until combine.
- Place a medium sized non-stick wok over medium-high flame, add 1 tablespoon oil and heat until hot. Add eggplant and zucchini slices in a single layer and cook for 3-5 minutes until nicely brown on all sides.
- Transfer vegetables to a separate plate and heat 1 tablespoon oil in wok. Cut each tempeh slice in half and add to batch in a single layer. Sprinkle with salt and paprika and pan-fry for 3-5 minutes or until it turns nicely golden brown.
- Transfer vegetables to a separate plate and wipe the pan clean.
- Cut mushrooms into thin slices, add to wok and roast for 5-8 minutes until mushrooms lose most of their moisture.
- Peel onion and cut into thin rings.
- Transfer dough onto a clean working space, dusted with flour. Pat dough and using a rolling pin, shape dough into 12-inch diameter round

crust. Roll crust, then unroll over prepared pizza pan and gently press it to the edges.

- Spread prepared tomato puree mixture, leave the 1-inch edge. Top with mushrooms, zucchini and eggplant slices, and then tempeh slices.
- Place pizza pan on oven and bake pizza for 15-20 minutes until vegetables are completely cooked through, and crust is nicely golden brown.
- Remove baked pizza from oven, let cool for 5 minutes and then slice to serve.

NUTRITIONAL INFORMATION PER SERVING:

242 Cal, 8.95 g total fat (3.5 g sat. fat), 10 mg chol., 546 mg sodium, 30.9 g carb., 1.9 g fiber, 9.33 g protein.

Cauliflower Crust Pizza

Grounded cauliflower makes a gluten-free base of this pizza. It goes best with any kind of toppings, feel free to experiment it.

Yield: About 1 pizza
Total Time: 60 minutes

INGREDIENTS

- 20.3 ounces / 575g cauliflower head
- 16 fluid ounces / 475ml water
- 1 egg
- 3 ounces / 100g grated Parmesan cheese
- ¼ teaspoon salt
- 2 tablespoons olive oil, divided
- 2 fluid ounces / 60ml tomato sauce
- 7 ounces / 200g grated Parmesan cheese
- 1 small red onion
- 1 medium tomato

2 ounces chopped cilantro
¼ teaspoon red chili flakes

DIRECTIONS

- Switch on the baking oven, set the temperature at 400 degrees F and let it preheat.
- Cut cauliflower into floret, place it in a food processor, pour in water and pulse until smooth. Using fine sieve strain mixture, transfer the mixture into a microwaveable bowl and microwave for 5 minutes on high heat setting.
- Transfer cauliflower mixture onto a clean dish towel and squeeze out all the liquid as much as possible until completely dry.
- Place cauliflower in a bowl, add egg, salt, cheese, 1 tablespoon oil and stir until mix well.
- Line a 14-inch pizza pan with baking paper, place cauliflower mixture into the center of the pan and use wet hands to pat the mixture into a round crust as thin as possible.
- Transfer the dough to a clean working space, dusted with flour. Pat dough using a rolling pin, shape dough into a 12-inch diameter round crust. Roll crust, then unroll over prepared pizza pan and gently press it to the edges.
- Drizzle remaining oil over crust and place pan into the oven to bake for 30 minutes until crust is nicely golden brown and crisp.
- In the meantime, cut tomato into thin slices. Peel onion and cut into thin rings.
- Remove pan from oven, leave the oven on, line crust with a parchment sheet and flip upside down, then remove parchment.

- Spread tomato sauce over crust, leave 1-inch edge, spread with cheese, tomato slices and onion rings.
- Place pan into the oven to bake for 20-22 minutes or until cheese melts completely and the top is brown.
- Remove baked pizza from oven, let cool for 5 minutes, garnish with cilantro, sprinkle with red chili flakes and slice to serve.

NUTRITIONAL INFORMATION PER SERVING:

170.3 Cal, 3.2g total fat (2.8 g sat. fat), 41.8 mg chol., 2501 mg sodium, 22.3 g carb., 2.8g fiber, 16 g protein.

Corn & Black Bean Pizza

Make a full meal by serving this meatless Mexican pizza with a side salad. It is loaded with fiber, vitamins and minerals.

Yield: About 1 pizza
Total Time: 30 minutes

INGREDIENTS
   1 large tomato
   6 ounces / 150g cooked black beans
   6 ounces / 150g fresh corn kernels
   2 tablespoons cornmeal

16 ounces / 450g frozen whole-wheat pizza dough, thawed
2 fluid ounces / 80ml barbecue sauce

DIRECTIONS

- Preheat grill.
- Chop tomato and place in a bowl. Add beans and corn and stir until it mixes well.
- Take a large baking sheet and sprinkle evenly with cornmeal.
- Transfer dough onto a clean working space, dusted with flour. Pat dough using rolling pin, shape dough into 12-inch diameter round crust. Roll crust and then unroll over cornmeal so that cornmeal covers the underside of the crust.
- Transfer crust to grill, cover and cook for 4-5 minutes or until crust puffs and bottom is nicely golden brown.
- Then carefully flip crust suing spatula, then quickly spread barbecue sauce evenly over crust, leave 1-inch edge, top with tomato mixture and cover with cheese.
- Return lid and cook for another 4-5 minute until cheese melts completely and the bottom is nicely golden brown.
- Remove baked pizza from oven, let cool for 5 minutes and then slice to serve.

NUTRITIONAL INFORMATION PER SERVING:

302 Cal, 9g total fat (3 g sat. fat), 15 mg chol., 484 mg sodium, 48 g carb., 4 g fiber, 13 g protein.

Beans & Spicy Mango Pizza

Beans and spicy mango pizza is a perfect summer pizza. Trying this pizza during family pizza nights is wonderful.

Yield: About 1 pizza
Total Time: 25 minutes

INGREDIENTS

- 1 medium zucchini
- 1 medium mango
- 16 ounces / 45g frozen pizza dough, thawed
- 8 ounces / 250g hot salsa
- 8 ounces / 250g shredded Mexican cheese blend
- 2 ounces / 50g cooked black beans
- 1 medium green onion
- 2 ounces / 50g cilantro leaves

DIRECTIONS

- Peel mango and zucchini and slice. Slice green onion.
- Switch on the baking oven, set the temperature at 400 degrees F and let it preheat.
- In the meantime, grease a 14-inch pizza pan with oil.
- Transfer dough onto a clean working space, dusted with flour. Pat dough using rolling pin, shape dough into a 12-inch diameter round crust. Roll crust, then unroll over prepared pizza pan and gently press it to the edges.
- Spread salsa evenly onto the crust, leave 1-inch edge. Top with Mexican cheese blend, zucchini and mango slices and beans.
- Place pan into the oven to bake for 15-20 minutes or until crust and top turns golden brown.
- Remove baked pizza from oven, let cool for 5 minutes, garnish with green onion and cilantro, and slice to serve.

NUTRITIONAL INFORMATION PER SERVING:

130 Cal, 4.8 g total fat (1.8 g sat. fat), 7.5 mg chol., 7.5 mg sodium, 14.8 g carb., 3g fiber, 6.4 g protein.

Artichoke, Broccoli and Spinach Pesto Pizza

This green, super healthy and nutritious pizza is loaded with the creamy spinach pesto with a hint of cheese, broccoli and artichoke heart and feta.

Yield: About 1 pizza
Total Time: 55 minutes

INGREDIENTS

2 ounces / 50g chopped walnuts
8 ounces / 200g spinach leaves
8 ounces / 200g basil leaves
2 teaspoons garlic
¾ teaspoon salt
¼ teaspoon ground black pepper
4 fluid ounces / 120ml olive oil
4 ounces / 100g grated Parmesan cheese
16 ounces / 450g frozen pizza dough, thawed
14 ounces / 350g artichoke hearts
18 ounces / 510g broccoli heads

16 ounces / 400g crumbled feta cheese

DIRECTIONS

- Switch on the baking oven, set the temperature at 425 degrees F and let it preheat.
- In the meantime, grease a 14-inch pizza pan with oil.
- Prepare spinach pesto. Place a small non-stick skillet pan over medium flame, add walnuts and cook for 3-5 minutes or until lightly toasted, stir often. Then remove walnuts from heat and let it cool.
- Place spinach, basil, garlic, walnuts Into a blender and pulse until minced.
- Add salt, black pepper, olive oil, cheese and pulse until it's smooth. Tip pesto into a bowl and set aside until needed,
- Cut broccoli into florets, place it in a microwaveable bowl and microwave for 3-5 minutes or until tender. Strain broccoli in a fine sieve to drain its liquid and set aside until cool.
- While broccoli cools off, transfer dough onto a clean working space, dusted with flour. Pat dough using a rolling pin, then shape dough into a 12-inch diameter round crust. Roll crust, then unroll over prepared pizza pan and gently press it to the edges.
- Spread evenly with prepared pesto, leave 1-inch edge. Sprinkle with ½ portion of feta and evenly top with broccoli. Quarter each artichoke and distribute evenly over broccoli layer.
- Sprinkle with remaining feta cheese and place pan into the oven to bake for 30-35 minutes or

until crust and top is nicely golden brown and vegetables are cooked through.
- Remove baked pizza from oven, let cool for 5 minutes and then slice to serve.

NUTRITIONAL INFORMATION PER SERVING:

283 Cal, 14 g total fat (4 g sat. fat), 19 mg chol., 512 mg sodium, 33 g carb., 3g fiber, 15 g protein.

Chocolate Pizza

One word for this pizza, heavenly! This unique chocolate pizza is an ultimate dessert and can also serve as a dessert to impress your love one or celebrate special occasions with it.

Yield: About 1 pizza
Total Time: 30 minutes

INGREDIENTS

- 16 ounces / 450g frozen pizza dough, thawed
- 2 teaspoons fat-free butter, melted
- 2 ounces / 60g chocolate hazelnut spread
- 3 ounces / 90g chocolate chips
- 2 tablespoons milk chocolate chips
- 2 tablespoons white chocolate chips
- 2 tablespoons chopped hazelnuts

DIRECTIONS

- Switch on the baking oven, set the temperature at 375 degrees F and let it preheat.
- In the meantime, grease a large baking tray with oil and set aside until needed.
- Transfer dough to a clean working space dusted with flour. Pat dough using rolling pin shape dough into 9-inch diameter round crust. Roll crust, then unroll over prepared baking tray using your fingers to make indentation all over the crust.
- Brush crust with butter and place baking tray in the oven to bake for 15-20 minutes until nicely golden brown.
- Remove crust from oven and immediately spread with hazelnut spread and sprinkle evenly with all the chocolate chips.
- Return pizza to oven and bake for another 1-2 minutes or until chocolate chips begin to melt.
- Remove baked pizza from oven, let cool for 5 minutes, garnish with hazelnuts and slice to serve.

NUTRITIONAL INFORMATION PER SERVING:

190 Cal, 11 g total fat (6 g sat. fat), 5 mg chol., 40 mg sodium, 21 g carb., 1 g fiber, 2 g protein.

Raspberry Brie Pizza

This Brie cheese pizza is unique and offers luxurious texture and extraordinary softness that pairs well with raspberry.

Yield: About 1 pizza
Total Time: 35 minutes

INGREDIENTS

8.5 ounces / 240g frozen wewalka bistro style pizza dough, thawed
2 tablespoons fat-free butter
5 ounces walnuts
¼ teaspoon ground cinnamon
2 tablespoons brown sugar
3 ounces brie cheese
1 tablespoon olive oil
3 ounces / 95g raspberry preserves
7 ounces / 200g fresh raspberries

1 teaspoon chopped rosemary

DIRECTIONS

- Switch on the baking oven, set the temperature at 400 degrees F and let it preheat.
- In the meantime, place a small saucepan over medium flame, add butter and heat for 2-3 minutes or until it melts. Add walnuts, cinnamon and sugar and stir to mix. Cook mixture for 4-5 minute or until sugar caramelizes. Then transfer the nut mixture to a wax paper, spread evenly and let it cool completely.
- Line a medium sized baking tray with parchment sheet and place pizza dough. Brush evenly with oil. Thinly slice brie cheese and arrange onto pizza dough and around each slice of cheese, drop a spoon of jam and then evenly arrange half of the raspberries.
- Sprinkle rosemary over pizza and place the baking tray into the oven.
- Bake pizza for 12-15 minutes until crust is nicely golden brown.
- Remove baked pizza from oven, let cool for 5 minutes, then garnish with remaining raspberries and walnuts mixture and slice to serve.

NUTRITIONAL INFORMATION PER SERVING:

281 Cal, 14 g total fat (5 g sat. fat), 45 mg chol., 205 mg sodium, 23 g carb., 2 g fiber, 16 g protein.

Meat Lover Pizzas

Chinese Chicken Hoisin Pizza

In this recipe, an Asian chicken pizza is present with a tasty twist that is chicken flavored with hoisin sauce.

Yield: About 1 pizza

Total Time: 40 minutes

INGREDIENTS

16 ounces / 450g frozen pizza dough, thawed
1 large white onion
6 medium green onions
7.5 ounces / 211g shredded cooked chicken
2 teaspoons minced garlic
1 tablespoon minced ginger
3 tablespoons hoisin sauce & more as needed
1 teaspoon Sambal Oelek
6.5 ounces / 181g fat-free shredded mozzarella cheese
2 ounces / 60.3g chopped cilantro

DIRECTIONS

- Switch on the baking oven, set the temperature at 500 degrees F and let it preheat.
- In the meantime, grease a 14-inch pizza pan with oil and set aside until needed.
- Peel green onions, cut diagonally into thin slice and place in a medium-sized bowl. Add shredded chicken in a bowl, add garlic, ginger, hoisin sauce, Sambal oelek and toss to coat well.
- Transfer dough onto a clean working space, dusted with flour. Pat dough using rolling pin, shape dough into 12-inch diameter round crust. Roll crust, then unroll over prepared pizza pan and gently press it to the edges.
- Spread ¼ cup hoisin sauce over crust, leave 1-inch edge.

- Peel white onion, slice and spread over crust and then top with chicken mixture. Cover with cheese and place pan into the oven.
- Bake pizza for 10-12 minutes or until crust is turns golden brown and top is brown.
- Cut remaining green onions diagonally into thin slices.
- Remove baked pizza from oven, let cool for 5 minutes, sprinkle with cilantro and then slice to serve.

NUTRITIONAL INFORMATION PER SERVING:

316 Cal, 14.5g total fat (6.8 g sat. fat), 80 mg chol., 786 mg sodium, 19.4 g carb., 2.2 g fiber, 26.6 g protein.

Chicken Garlic Pizza

Impress family by baking this chicken garlic pizza that taste exactly like the restaurant one and turns out in less than 30 minutes.

Yield: About 1 pizza
Total Time: 25 minutes

INGREDIENTS

1 big tomato
6 ounces / 170g chicken breast, grilled
16 ounces / 450g frozen pizza dough, thawed
6 ounces / 170g ranch dressing
1 tablespoon minced garlic
12 ounces / 340g fat-free shredded mozzarella cheese
2 ounces / 60g grated non-fat cheddar cheese
1.5 ounces / 45g grated Parmesan cheese
2 ounces / 15g chopped green onions

DIRECTIONS

- Switch on the baking oven, set temperature at 425 degrees F and let it preheat.
- In the meantime, grease a 14-inch pizza pan with oil.
- Transfer dough onto a clean working space, dusted with flour. Pat dough using rolling pin shape dough into 12-inch diameter round crust. Roll crust, then unroll over prepared pizza pan and gently press it to the edges.
- In a medium bowl stir together ranch dressing and garlic until mix well and then spread dressing evenly on the crust, leave 1-inch edge.
- In another medium sized bowl combine all the cheeses and then evenly spread half of the mixture over sauce layer on the crust.
- Slice chicken and arrange on cheese layer. Dice tomato and scatter over chicken layer and top with green onion. Cover with remaining cheeses mixture and place pan into the oven.
- Bake pizza for 12-15 minutes until the cheese melts and the crust and top are nicely golden brown.
- Remove baked pizza from oven, let it cool for 5 minutes and then slice to serve.

NUTRITIONAL INFORMATION PER SERVING:

320 Cal, 15 g total fat (6 g sat. fat), 35 mg chol., 600 mg sodium, 30 g carb., 1 g fiber, 18 g protein.

Chicken, Bacon & Strawberry Pizza

This unique pizza accompanies flavorful chicken and smoked bacon in addition to the fresh strawberry and plenty of cheese.

Yield: About 1 pizza
Total Time: 40 minutes

INGREDIENTS

4 ounces / 120g strawberry Jam
2 fluid ounces / 60ml apple cider vinegar

1 teaspoon Sriracha Sauce
16 ounces / 45g frozen pizza dough, thawed
6 ounces / 170g chicken breast, cooked
4 ounces / 110g smoked bacon
1 medium sweet onion
12 ounces / 340g Italian cheese blend
2 ounces / 50g cilantro
2 ounces / 50g Fresh strawberries

DIRECTIONS

- Switch on the baking oven, set temperature at 450 degrees F and let it preheat.
- In the meantime, grease a 14-inch pizza pan with oil.
- Place a small saucepan over medium flame, pour vinegar and bring to boil. Then reduce heat and simmer vinegar for 4-5 minutes or until it reduces to half and consistency is thick and syrupy.
- Remove saucepan from the flame, add jam and Sriracha, stir until combine and set aside until cool.
- While mixture cools off, transfer the dough onto a clean working space, dusted with flour. Pat dough using rolling pin, shape dough into a 12-inch diameter round crust. Roll crust, then unroll over prepared pizza pan and gently press it to the edges.
- Dice chicken, place in a bowl, add 2 tablespoons of prepared raspberry mixture and toss to coat completely.
- Onto pizza crust, spread remaining cooked raspberry mixture, leave the 1-inch edge. Top

evenly with chicken mixture and then cover with ¾ portion of cheese.

- Cut bacon into bite size pieces. Peel and thinly slice onion.
- Arrange bacon over cheese layer, followed by onion slices and then sprinkle with remaining cheese.
- Place pan in the oven to bake for 10-12 minutes or until crust and top is nicely golden brown and cheese bubbles.
- Remove baked pizza from oven, let cool for 5 minutes.
- Dice strawberries and scatter over pizza, sprinkle with cilantro and then slice to serve.

NUTRITIONAL INFORMATION PER SERVING:

270 Cal, 7 g total fat (3 g sat. fat), 90 mg chol., 250 mg sodium, 28 g carb., 3 g fiber, 19 g protein.

Meatball Pizza

Meatball pizza is a quick fix meal. Always store an extra dough and frozen meatballs and make this filling pizza any time of the day.

Yield: About 1 pizza
Total Time: 30 minutes

INGREDIENTS

16 ounces / 450g frozen pizza dough, thawed
8 ounces / 235g pizza sauce
1 teaspoon garlic powder
1 teaspoon Italian seasoning
1 small red onion
12 frozen meatballs, thawed
2 ounces / 60g grated Parmesan cheese
8 ounces / 240g fat-free shredded mozzarella cheese

DIRECTIONS

- Switch on the baking oven, set the temperature at 350 degrees F and let it preheat.
- In the meantime, grease a 14-inch pizza pan with oil.
- Transfer dough onto a clean working space, dusted with flour. Pat dough using rolling pin, shape the dough into a 12-inch diameter round crust. Roll crust, then unroll over prepared pizza pan and gently press it to the edges.
- Spread pizza sauce evenly on the crust, leave 1-inch edge, and sprinkle with Italian seasoning, garlic and parmesan cheese.
- Peel onion, cut in half, slice and scatter over crust. Arrange meatballs and cover with mozzarella cheese
- Sprinkle cheese over crust and place pan into the oven to bake for 10-12 minutes or until crust and top is nicely golden brown.
- Remove baked pizza from oven, let cool for 5 minutes and then slice to serve.

NUTRITIONAL INFORMATION PER SERVING:

280 Cal, 10 g total fat (5 g sat. fat), 25 mg chol., 710 mg sodium, 33 g carb., 1 g fiber, 15 g protein.

Pizza Cubano

All the flavors of a cubano sandwich are present in the pizza form. Flavor full mustard paste, tender chicken, crispy ham, tangy pickles and off course cheese, all in one pizza.

Yield: About 1 pizza
Total Time: 30 minutes

INGREDIENTS
- 1 small red onion
- 1 dill pickle
- 16 ounces / 450g frozen pizza dough, thawed
- 2 tablespoons yellow mustard
- 3 ounces / 85g chicken breast, cooked
- 2 ounces / 60g baked ham
- 4 ounces / 120g parsley
- 3 ounces / 85g grated Gruyere cheese

DIRECTIONS

- Switch on the baking oven, set the temperature at 375 degrees F and let it preheat.
- In the meantime, grease a 14-inch pizza pan with oil.
- Peel onion and chop. Chop pickle, shred chicken and thinly slice ham.
- Now, prepare the crust. Transfer dough onto a clean working space, dusted with flour. Pat dough using a rolling pin, shape dough into a 12-inch diameter round crust. Roll crust, then unroll over prepared pizza pan and gently press it to the edges.
- Spread mustard paste over crust, leave the 1-inch edge, sprinkle with pickle and then onion. Arrange with shredded chicken and ham. Scatter with parsley and cover with cheese.
- Place pan in the oven to bake for 12-15 minutes or until crust and top is nicely golden brown.
- Remove baked pizza from oven, let cool for 5 minutes and then slice to serve.

NUTRITIONAL INFORMATION PER SERVING:

260 Cal, 4.8 g total fat (1.7 g sat. fat), 48 mg chol., 560 mg sodium, 38 g carb., 6.4 g fiber, 22 g protein.

Pepperoni & Cheese Tortilla Pizza

In absence of a pizza crust, feel free to use a tortilla as a pizza base. Tortilla pizzas are much healthier and faster than the take-out ones.

Yield: About 1 pizza
Total Time: 25 minutes

INGREDIENTS

  1 large floured tortilla
  4 ounces / 120g pizza sauce
  2 ounces / 120g shredded fat-free cheddar cheese
  6 pepperoni pieces

DIRECTIONS

- Switch on the baking oven, set the temperature at 375 degrees F and let it preheat.

- Grease a cookie sheet with oil and place tortilla bread. Spread half of the pizza sauce evenly over bread and then sprinkle with cheese.
- Arrange pepperoni over cheese layer and place sheet in oven to bake for 5-8 minutes or until cheese melts completely and the edges begin to crusty.
- Remove baked pizza from oven, let cool for 5 minutes and then slice to serve.

NUTRITIONAL INFORMATION PER SERVING:

247 Cal, 8.5 g total fat (2.9 g sat. fat), 16 mg chol., 611 mg sodium, 30.8 g carb., 5 g fiber, 12 g protein.

Avocado & Salmon Tortilla Pizza

This tortilla pizza is a light healthy pizza that is perfect for brunch or snack.

Yield: About 1 pizza
Total Time: 30 minutes

INGREDIENTS

    1 floured tortilla
    4 tablespoons fat-free cream cheese
    ½ tablespoon dried basil
    1 teaspoon minced garlic
    1 tablespoon olive oil
    1 small red onion
    3.5 ounces / 100g fat-free shredded mozzarella cheese
    3.5 ounces / 100g smoked salmon
    1 small avocado
    ¼ teaspoon lemon pepper

DIRECTIONS

- Switch on the baking oven, set the temperature at 400 degrees F and let it preheat.
- In a bowl, place cream cheese and using electric mixer combine with garlic and dill until mix well.
- Grease a cookie sheet with oil and place tortilla bread.
- Brush crust with oil, then spread with cream cheese mixture.
- Peel onion, cut into rings and scatter over tortilla and then cover with cheese.
- Place pan into the oven to bake for 10-12 minutes or until the cheese melts completely and the crust and top are nicely golden brown.
- Remove baked pizza from oven and let cool for 5 minutes, do not switch off oven.
- In the meantime, slice salmon. Peel the avocado and slice thinly.
- Arrange salmon slices on the pizza, then top it with avocado and sprinkle lemon pepper.
- Return pizza to oven and bake for 2-3 minutes until warm through.
- Remove pizza and slice to serve.

NUTRITIONAL INFORMATION PER SERVING:

236 Cal, 12 g total fat (1.9 g sat. fat), 45 mg chol., 519 mg sodium, 27 g carb., 4.5 g fiber, 18.8 g protein.

Shrimp & Basil Pesto Pizza

A tasty combination of creamy pesto pizza, shrimps and garden vegetables make a wonderful sea-food pizza.

Yield: About 1 pizza
Total Time: 25 minutes

INGREDIENTS
1 small red onion
2 small fresh tomatoes
3 ounces / 85g shrimps, grilled
4 ounces / 120g grated Parmesan cheese
4 ounces / 110g frozen pizza dough, thawed
2 tablespoons olive oil
½ teaspoon salt
¼ teaspoon ground black pepper
2 tablespoons basil pesto

DIRECTIONS

- Peel onion and cut into thin rings. Slice tomatoes.
- Set up the grill, heat grilling rack over medium-high flame and grease the grilling rack with oil generously.
- In the meantime, transfer the dough onto a clean working space dusted with flour. Pat dough using rolling pin, shape dough into a 10-inch diameter round crust. Brush one side of crust with olive oil and then season with salt and black pepper.
- Gently place crust on the grilling rack, oiled side down and then brush the other side with oil. Cook crust for 2-3 minutes or until underside crust is lightly charred, and then flip crust. Cook for another 1-2 minutes and then slide crust to the cool side of grilling rack.
- Immediately spread pesto over crust, leave 1-inch edge, scatter with shrimps and then with tomato and onion slices and cover with cheese. Cover grill and cook pizza for 3-5 minutes until vegetables are tender and cheese melts completely.
- Remove pizza from grill, let cool for 5 minutes and then slice to serve.

NUTRITIONAL INFORMATION PER SERVING:

234 Cal, 12 g total fat (3.6 g sat. fat), 31 mg chol., 521 mg sodium, 20 g carb., 2 g fiber, 14 g protein.

Chicken & Bacon-Basil Pesto Pizza

This easy dinner pizza accompanies combination chicken and bacon pesto that serve as a great meal.

Yield: About 1 pizza
Total Time: 45 minutes

INGREDIENTS

16 ounces / 450g frozen pizza dough, thawed
17 ounces / 500g basil leaves
2 teaspoons minced garlic
8 bacon slices, uncooked
3 ounces / 90g grated Parmesan cheese
4 fluid ounces / 120ml olive oil
5 ounces / 140g fat-free shredded mozzarella cheese
6 ounces / 170g chicken breast, uncooked
¼ teaspoon ground black pepper

DIRECTIONS

- Switch on the baking oven, set the temperature at 425 degrees F and let it preheat.
- In the meantime, grease a 14-inch pizza pan with oil.
- Place a medium sized non-stick skillet pan over medium flame, heat 1 tablespoon oil and fry bacon in batches until nicely golden brown on all sides and cook through.
- Transfer cooked bacon to a cutting board, let it cool slightly and then chop half of the bacon, reserve remaining bacon for topping pizza.
- Wipe clean pan, add chicken breast and cook for 7-10 minutes until tender. Then transfer chicken breast to a cutting board using fork shred meat. Set aside until required.
- Now prepare pesto. In a blender place basil and garlic and pulse until it minces. Add cheese and pulse until it combines. Continue processing and blend in oil until it incorporates and becomes smooth. Tip mixture into a bowl add chopped cooked bacon and stir until it mixes .
- Transfer dough onto a clean working space, dusted with flour. Pat dough using rolling pin, shape dough into 12-inch diameter round crust. Roll crust, then unroll over prepared pizza pan and gently press it to the edges.
- Spread bacon-basil pesto evenly, leave 1-inch edge, then cover with cheese and scatter with cooked bacon slices and chicken.
- Sprinkle black pepper over pizza and place pan into the oven to bake for 15-20 minutes or until crust and top is nicely golden brown.

- Remove baked pizza from oven, let cool for 5 minutes and then slice to serve.

NUTRITIONAL INFORMATION PER SERVING:

271 Cal, 5.1 g total fat (2.3 g sat. fat), 65 mg chol., 560 mg sodium, 38 g carb., 6.4 g fiber, 22 g protein.

Chicken-Broccoli Garlic Bread Pizza

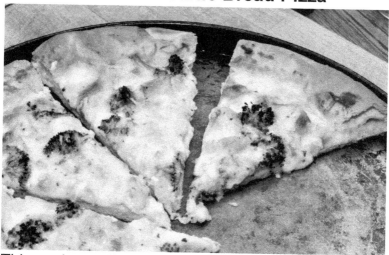

This recipe calls for garlic bread crust topped with chicken and broccoli, boosted with the flavors of Alfredo sauce and off course cheese.

Yield: About 1 pizza
Total Time: 70 minutes

INGREDIENTS

- 8 fluid ounces / 250ml water, warm
- 1 ¼ teaspoons dry-active yeast
- ½ teaspoon sugar
- 11 ounces / 300g all-purpose flour
- 1 teaspoon garlic powder
- ½ teaspoon dried basil
- ½ teaspoon salt
- 2 tablespoons grated Parmesan cheese
- 6 ounces chicken breast
- ½ teaspoon salt
- ¼ teaspoon ground black pepper
- 4 ounces / 120g Alfredo Sauce

12 ounces / 350g broccoli florets
12 ounces / 350g fat-free shredded mozzarella cheese
3 tablespoons grated Parmesan cheese

DIRECTIONS

- Switch on the baking oven, set the temperature at 425 degrees F and let it preheat.
- Grease a 14-inch pizza pan with oil and set aside until required.
- Pour warm water in a small bowl, stir in yeast and sugar and set aside in a warm place for 5-10 minutes or until foamy.
- Using a stand mixer, place flour, garlic, basil, salt and cheese and combine all the ingredients at medium speed. Turn mixer to low speed and slowly mix yeast mixer until firm dough comes together. Mix 1-2 tablespoons flour if the dough is too sticky or mix 1-2 tablespoons water is dough is too dry.
- Transfer dough onto a clean working space, dusted with flour and kneaded dough for 5 minutes. Shape dough into a ball, place in a bowl, cover with a wet towel and let it stand in a warm place for 30-45 minutes until dough doubles in size.
- In the meantime, prepared chicken. Season chicken with salt and black pepper. Place a non-stick skillet pan over a medium flame, heat 1 tablespoon oil and place chicken. Cook chicken for 7-10 minutes or until tender and then transfer to a cutting board.
- Let chicken cool slightly and then make use of a fork shred.

- Transfer dough onto a clean working space, pat dough using a rolling pin, shape dough into a 12-inch diameter round crust. Roll crust, then unroll over prepared pizza pan and gently press it to the edges.
- Place pan into the oven to bake for 5 minutes or until crust is nicely golden brown. Remove pan from oven and immediately spread with Alfredo sauce, leave 1-inch edge. Scatter with chicken and then with broccoli. Sprinkle with cheese and return pan to oven.
- Bake pizza for 12-15 minutes until the top is nicely golden brown and cheese bubbles.
- Remove baked pizza from oven, let cool for 5 minutes and then slice to serve.

NUTRITIONAL INFORMATION PER SERVING:

380 Cal, 22 g total fat (8 g sat. fat), 25 mg chol., 680 mg sodium, 35 g carb., 2 g fiber, 14 g protein.

CPSIA information can be obtained
at www.ICGtesting.com
Printed in the USA
LVHW081303310120
645453LV00013B/592